# HELP!

# HE'S STRUGGLING WITH PORNOGRAPHY

Brian Croft

Consulting Editor: Dr. Paul Tautges

© Day One Publications 2010

First printed 2010
Reprinted 2011

ISBN 978-1-84625-218-1

Published by Day One Publications
Ryelands Road, Leominster, HR6 8NZ

TEL 01568 613 740 FAX 01568 611 473

email—sales@dayone.co.uk

UK web site—www.dayone.co.uk

USA web site—www.dayonebookstore.com

Designed by **documen**
Printed by Orchard Press (Cheltenham) Ltd

To my dear courageous friends,
Jim and Linda:
May you continue to walk in
the grace and victory you have
found through the gospel and the
local church.

A special thanks to:
Jason Adkins, Adam Embry,
Scott Croft, and Scott Wells for
your helpful suggestions with
this manuscript;
Josh Hayward, for your insight and
assistance with the "Putting Off
Sin & Putting On Christ" chart.

# Contents

You may be reading this booklet for one of any number of reasons. Perhaps you know someone struggling in this battle and you want to help him. Or you may be the one who needs the help. This booklet may interest you solely because the word "pornography" caught your eye, and it has caused you to thumb through it to see what juicy issues might be discussed. Whatever your reasons, I hope you will consider the important ones that compelled me to write this booklet.

First and most obvious is the consuming presence of sexual perversion in our culture fueled by this gross form of entertainment. Through this multibillion-dollar industry lives are wrecked and marriages are destroyed, and its constant influence affects our daily lives. Thus we must be equipped to know how to face it, deal with its influence, and walk in victory from its clutches.

A second reason is the quality of resources currently available. Though several books have tackled the destructive issues surrounding a bondage to pornography, some diagnose the problem well, while others may miss the root problem but give good practical advice for the daily fight. My prayer for this booklet is that the fundamental issue will be clearly and biblically diagnosed, a hopeful solution will be presented, and practical ways to walk in victory over this bondage will empower those seeking help.

Additionally, I have a few personal reasons for taking on this project. It is staggering to realize how many issues I have dealt with as a pastor that directly relate to the allurements, bondages, and destructive patterns that come with a struggle with pornography. What you will find in these pages is the process that I and my fellow pastors walk through with men in my church— whether married, single, young or old—and that has proven to be incredibly fruitful and effective, by God's grace, over the years. My hope is that it will prove the same for your loved one, perhaps you yourself, your pastors, and your local church.

Finally, and most personally, this struggle once gripped me for many years. I was exposed to pornography at a young age and that led to a bondage that followed me throughout my teen years and into college. I gladly yet fearfully took on this booklet because the biblical truths that anchor the process to overcome this struggle brought amazing help and freedom in my own life. Please read on, and may you or your loved one be helped as I have been.

*Brian Croft*
*Senior Pastor*
*Auburndale Baptist Church*
*Louisville, Kentucky, USA*

# INTRODUCTION

We are living in an unprecedented time. Pornographic images and sexually explicit material are more readily available right now than at any other time in history. This is confirmed at the shopping malls we walk through, the billboards we drive past, the "retail" catalogs mailed to our homes, and the magazine racks at the store. The estimated financial size of the worldwide sex industry is around $57 billion, with $12 billion (just over 20 percent) coming from the United States.[1] The reality of pornography's influence is more painfully known through the marriages destroyed by it, the pastors shamed and fired because of it, and the people victimized by the sexually related crimes we hear reported on the news almost every day.

1 William M. Struthers, *Wired for Intimacy: How Pornography Hijacks the Male Brain* (Downers Grove, IL: Intervarsity Press, 2009), 20.

Possibly the most sobering effect of this trend is the way it has so deeply affected Christians within the local church. Place the most skilled fireman alone in a burning building where he is surrounded by flames and never relieved, and he will eventually get burned. Similarly, though we as Christians have been transformed by faith in the person and work of our Savior Jesus, we too have been harmed as a result of being immersed in this sex-saturated culture. How do we as Christians find lasting victory over this struggle and help others to do the same?

We first find victory through the transforming power of the gospel. Regardless of the kind of bondage to sin we face, only repenting of our sins and trusting in the person and work of Jesus Christ can bring the lasting freedom that we seek. A common flaw in dealing with the sinful patterns of viewing sexually explicit material is to focus solely on employing methods to stop the behavior (behavior modification) to the exclusion of addressing the root issues of the heart. True, genuine, and lasting change in this struggle, or in any struggle with sin, must begin on the inside. The inward change will bring the lasting change in our behavior.

We must also be wholly committed to the local church if we are to find lasting victory over this struggle. A further common flaw in trying to break the cycle of pornography is to think that one or two random accountability partners are enough. Daily walking in victory over this struggle requires a community effort and an accountability that stretches far beyond a Christian co-worker asking a man questions once a week regarding which Internet sites he has visited. The victory comes as spiritual guidance, care, rebuke, and marriage counseling are given by the man's leaders; when those most committed to the man's spiritual maturity (other church members) pray for him and his struggle; when the man's accountability partner reports to his pastors and spouse (if he is married) on his progress in this battle, and the man feels the looming presence of church discipline in response to the seriousness of his sin; when more is at stake than merely disappointing an accountability partner who has probably been chosen because of his sympathy with this struggle. Without the close involvement of the local church, few find lasting victory from any sin and live the victorious life Christ purchased for us with his own life.

God's power works through the gospel in the local church so that a true and lasting victory is found over a struggle with pornography and true healing and forgiveness can be experienced. I pray that you are convinced of the same as you read these pages.

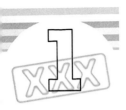

# The Problem: A Defiled Heart

The most insightful and well-thought-out solution will be meaningless if the problem is misdiagnosed. Let's begin by acknowledging what is *not* the problem before we focus on what *is*. The bondage of pornography is not gender-biased. Now more than ever, women too are lured to expose their minds to those images for the purpose of self-gratification. The struggle is not the result of a strong and active sex drive. The struggle cannot be blamed on a failed relationship with someone or on parents who failed to love us as they should have done. Though it is a factor in the struggle, the blame cannot even be placed on the easy accessibility of the Internet, television, movies, and inappropriate magazines resting at eye-level at the store. All these issues can contribute to the struggle, but none of them is the true root of the problem.

The fundamental problem is that our hearts are not right, a condition that dates back to the Garden of Eden. God created the heavens, the earth, and all the living creatures (Genesis 1–2). He also created man and woman in his image (Genesis 1:27), and they were united in one flesh, naked, and not ashamed (Genesis 2:24–25). God saw that all that he had made was very good (Genesis 1:31). Yet Adam and Eve sinned by disobeying God's word, eating of the tree of the knowledge of good and evil (Genesis 3:6). God told Adam and Eve not to eat from this tree or they would die (Genesis 2:17), yet Satan tempted Eve, and she ate from the tree and gave some of its fruit to her husband (Genesis 3:6). Instead of obeying God's command, they rebelled against him. They wanted to rule, not be ruled by God.

As a result, sin entered the world and affected everything in it, including all those born from Adam and Eve. Since they were the first human beings, everyone born after them has inherited their sinful heart. Therefore, all people born into this sinful world are born with defiled hearts that have a natural disposition to rebel against God and pursue the pleasures of sin. Our sinful behavior, related to sexual sin or otherwise, can be blamed on one thing and one thing only—our defiled hearts.

Jesus affirmed this. Mark 7:1–23 describes a confrontation that Jesus had with the Pharisees, who were arrogantly putting their faith in their deeds and traditions. They were blinded to what Jesus said really mattered to God—not the external, physical things we do, but the internal, spiritual matters of the heart. In this context, Jesus spoke the following profound words, not just about the corrupt state of our hearts, but also about how our hearts affect our relationship with God. Jesus stated that what goes into a man from the outside does not defile him because it does not go into his heart but into his stomach (vv.18–19). He continued,

> That which proceeds out of the man,
> that is what defiles the man. For from
> within, out of the heart of men, proceed
> the evil thoughts, fornications, thefts,
> murders, adulteries, deeds of coveting and
> wickedness, as well as deceit, sensuality,
> envy, slander, pride and foolishness. All
> these evil things proceed from within and
> defile the man.
>
> (vv. 20–23)

What an amazing insight for his Jewish disciples

who, for most of their lives, followed strict laws and traditions that said defilement came from foods and other objects declared unclean! Yet the Gospel accounts record that Jesus's consistent teaching was that the kingdom of God is based not on the external but on the internal—the heart.

Our defiled hearts are recognized by the evil actions that flow out from them. Imagine walking up to a giant apple tree with the anticipation of finding big juicy red apples, only to find that most of the apples are puny and rotten. There would be but one conclusion. Though we cannot see the roots and what is going on inside the tree, by observing the kind of fruit it produces we know the tree is sick. Similarly, we cannot see the defilement in our hearts, yet Jesus's teaching shows that something corrupt and sinful exists in our hearts because of the sin and corruption that proceed out of them.

Jesus also listed the sins that proceed out of the defiled heart in verses 21 and 22. There are sins of a *sexual nature* (fornication, adultery, sensuality), sins that *hurt others* (theft, murder, slander), and sins of *blatant self-regard* (covetousness, pride, envy). Part of this list also connects to the *Ten Commandments* (theft, murder, adultery, covetousness). Mark's list is for his readers to feel the weight of corruption that proceeds from and condemns the heart of man.

Jesus not only identified the problem, but he also demonstrated its seriousness:

> All these evil things proceed from within
> and defile the man.
>
> (v. 23)

The solution to this defilement is not as simple as going through a ceremony to clean our hands (vv. 1–5). It does not help to simply abstain from eating certain foods (v. 19). The situation is much more serious, because our defilement is so engrained in our natures that, even before we can train the smallest child to speak or walk, he or she already shows symptoms of this condition. It is so serious that we cannot stop ourselves from speaking hurtful words to the ones we love the most. It is so serious that we cannot keep ourselves from desiring that which we cannot have, though we already possess so much. It is so serious that we can become enslaved to a particular sin, such as pornography, all the while knowing it is wrong, unfulfilling, and will destroy us. This corruption is so serious that we are unable to do anything in our own power to change it.

Jesus's teaching is clear. Our longing for the sexual

perversion and pleasure of pornography is not due to what we are exposed to, ingest, or experience through life's hurtful circumstances. Our problem is that our hearts are defiled, and we cannot fix them or repair the damage ourselves. We need new hearts. The hope for receiving a new heart will be the topic of Chapter 3. For now, let us turn to the unique consequences that often accompany this destructive struggle.

# The Consequences: Wrecked Lives

No one would dispute that unavoidable consequences result from sin. Sin is first and foremost against God. Our defiled hearts, enmity with God, and potentially eternal separation from God are all consequences of rebelling against our Creator. Sin is also often committed against others. All of us in some way or another have felt the sting of sin through consequences such as physical pain, scarred relationships, and sometimes legal ramifications. Even though many consequences leave a painful reminder of the effects of sin, few consequences of sin sting like those that accompany sexual sin against others. Marriages are betrayed, churches are wounded, families are destroyed, and individual lives are held in bondage, all because of the destructive nature of this particular sin.

These consequences are not unique to our time. The consequences of sexual sin have throughout history had a deep, destructive, and life-altering effect on all who have fallen into its clutches. Even King David, described as a man after God's own heart (1 Samuel 13:14), was not immune to this temptation and reaping its disastrous consequences. To begin with, his having multiple wives violated God's command to have one wife (Genesis 2:24). He was a man who easily satisfied his lusts. One particular example is found in 2 Samuel 11, when David walked on the roof of his house and saw a woman bathing:

> Now when evening came David arose from
> his bed and walked around on the roof of
> the king's house, and from the roof he saw
> a woman bathing; and the woman was very
> beautiful in appearance. So David sent and
> inquired about the woman. And one said,
> "Is this not Bathsheba, the daughter of
> Eliam, the wife of Uriah the Hittite?"
>
> (2 Samuel 11:2–3)

David's journey down this road began as it does for many—with his eyes. He saw this woman, and though he had access to many beautiful women, he wanted more. If David had looked away and refused his initial desire, the consequences would have been lesser. Yet David couldn't control his eyes and so acted upon his lustful desire:

> David sent messengers and took her, and
> when she came to him, he lay with her;
> and when she had purified herself from her
> uncleanness, she returned to her house. The
> woman conceived; and she sent and told
> David, and said, "I am pregnant."
>
> (vv. 4–5)

When the pregnancy was reported to him he naively thought he could cover it up by a series of lies and betrayals. Little by little David was drawn into greater and graver sin. He ultimately killed Bathsheba's husband, Uriah (v. 17), and took Bathsheba as his wife (v. 27), confident that his sin would not be found out.

David's sad story teaches us that sin is committed not just against others, but ultimately against God, from whom no sin can be hidden. This reality was made especially clear for David when the Lord sent Nathan the prophet to confront him about his sin

19

(2 Samuel 12). Nathan told a parable that indicted David as the man who had committed this grievous sin against those for whom he was to care and over whom he was to rule justly. We find the consequences of David's sin against God and those he harmed in this powerful word from God through Nathan:

> "Now therefore, the sword shall never depart from your house, because you have despised Me and have taken the wife of Uriah the Hittite to be your wife." Thus says the LORD, "Behold, I will raise up evil against you from your own household; I will even take your wives before your eyes and give them to your companion, and he will lie with your wives in broad daylight. Indeed you did it secretly, but I will do this thing before all Israel, and under the sun." Then David said to Nathan, "I have sinned against the LORD." And Nathan said to David, "The LORD also has taken away your sin; you shall not die. However, because by this deed you have given occasion to the enemies of the LORD to blaspheme, the child also that is born to you shall surely die."
>
> (2 Samuel 12:10–14)

Though the Lord showed David mercy because he confessed his sin, God did not spare him the consequences of his adultery and murder, including the death of his illegitimate child. Much can be observed from this tragic account, but one observation is certain: regardless of who you are, where you come from, or what position of power you hold, the consequences of sexual sin will be fierce and inevitable. Although the sexual sin of pornography has grave consequences for everyone, those consequences become increasingly serious as one's role of spiritual accountability for others increases. The remainder of this chapter will highlight these consequences as they affect three groups: single men, married men, and pastors.

## The Single Man

One of the most obvious consequences for a single man is that pornography perverts his understanding of God's good purpose for sex in marriage. God said that it is not good for man to be alone (Genesis 2:18). Man has a God-given desire to have a helper, companion, and lover in a wife, and this desire is good. Specifically, sexual desires from this one-flesh union (Genesis 2:24) are to be fulfilled and enjoyed

21

solely and completely in a wife (Proverbs 5:19). Yet, if a man continually fills his mind and heart with a perversion of God's truth, as viewing pornography does, he will eventually believe and apply that perversion. Pornography causes men to see women simply as objects for their own pleasure and not as beautiful human beings who are to be cherished, honored, and respected. The longer a man exposes himself to an evil, selfish perversion of God's design for sex, the more likely that man will bring that understanding into bed with his future wife and not experience what God has intended for a husband and wife.[2] This misunderstanding also inevitably leads to the naivety of most men who think that this struggle will suddenly vanish once they are married.

Another harmful consequence of a single man's struggle is the deep frustration and discontentment that ultimately accompany any attempt to allow sin to replace that which only God can satisfy. C. S. Lewis affirmed this truth: "All that we call human history—money, poverty, ambition, war,

---

2  An entire book of the Bible (Song of Solomon) is dedicated to the enjoyment and pleasure that is to be experienced between a husband and wife within the confines of marital intimacy.

prostitution, classes, empires, slavery—[is] the long terrible story of man trying to find something other than God which will make him happy."[3]

If a single man seeks satisfaction in pornography and masturbation instead of in Christ, he will be in bondage to sin's empty promises and will never experience the joy that only comes from walking with the Savior and treasuring him most.

## The Married Man

The most obvious and harmful consequence for the married man who views pornography is the devastating betrayal of his wife and the covenant of marriage he has made to her before God. It needs to be recognized that viewing pornography and committing the physical act of adultery are not the same thing. In a married man's mind, they are not even in the same category. For the wife, however, the betrayal is stunningly similar. The harmful effects on the wife and on the marriage relationship are likely to be similar as well. The wife doubts her husband's physical attraction to her. The marriage bed is perceived as polluted. Trust on all levels is broken.

3  C. S. Lewis, *Mere Christianity* (New York: Macmillan, 1952), 53–54.

If a married man keeps his pornography struggle a secret from his wife (which most try and are able to do for a while), these same consequences escalate to an even greater level once the struggle is exposed.

As destructive as this consequence is, it does not match the destructiveness of how the gospel is perverted when a married man engages with pornography. The apostle Paul writes that a Christian husband's love for his wife is to be a display of Christ's love for his church in the way he gave his own life for her (Ephesians 5:25). When a man seeks satisfaction in pornography, therefore, he betrays and hurts his wife in such a way that it displays Christ as a selfish, unloving adulterer. Our enemy, the devil, wins an especially harmful victory when he targets married men and seduces them through sexual sin, because this perversion so distorts the gospel to a watching world.

## The Pastor

Speaking of enemy targets, the pastor is on the front line of attack and he seems to be specifically targeted by Satan in the area of sexual sin. According to a survey conducted by *Christianity Today* in 2000, "37 percent of pastors said pornography is a 'current struggle' of theirs. Fifty-seven percent called pornography the most sexually damaging issue for their congregations."[4] Undoubtedly, those numbers have increased in the last ten years. The enemy is cunning and has discovered a brilliant way to destroy marriages, ministries, local churches, and ultimately the message of the gospel by one single means— luring pastors into sexual sin. All these devastating consequences occur when a pastor who struggles with sexual sin is exposed.

The consequences resulting from sexual sin are undeniable and devastating, and the lives that are wrecked by it are often unrecoverable. Now more than ever we must know the solution to this epidemic and cling to it as our only hope.

4   Cited by Amy Frykholm, "Addictive Behavior: Pastors and Pornography," September 4, 2007, at The Christian Century: http://www.christiancentury.org/article.lasso?id=3629.

# The Solution: A New Heart

If the problem of pornography is that our hearts are naturally defiled, and if their corruption is so serious that we are unable to do anything in our own power to change them, then there is only one way to overcome this bondage. We need new hearts. In our era of medical technology, doctors can give us a heart transplant by physically taking out our old heart and putting in a new one. Yet Jesus says another kind of heart transplant is needed, one that the most gifted doctor cannot perform and that all the good deeds in the world cannot compensate for. A new heart must be supernaturally given by God himself.

Though the problem is immense and the consequences are devastating, the one true living God of the universe has the power to change the most defiled of hearts, place a new heart within a man, and empower him to walk through life in victory over sin. The provision of this new heart is revealed in the unfolding of redemptive history in the Bible. The only way to walk in lasting victory over sin, including the snare of pornography and sexual sin, is through receiving a new heart that can only be found through the gospel.

## A New Heart is *Promised* in the New Covenant

Through Moses, God made a covenant with his chosen people, Israel. It was a covenant with the promise of blessings for obedience and curses for disobedience (Deuteronomy 28). Although Israel declared that they would obey all that the Lord commanded (Exodus 24:3, 7), generation after generation forgot the Lord and betrayed the covenant. As a result, God brought the curses for disobedience that were promised, which becomes an unfortunate theme of most of the Old Testament.

Yet, in the midst of the unfaithfulness of his people, God showed faithfulness to them. Though they suffered under the curse of sin and disobedience to the covenant, God promised through the prophets that he would redeem them, save them from the curse of sin, and cause them to walk in his ways. The prophet Ezekiel declared that this redemption would come in the form of a new heart:

> For I will take you from the nations, gather you from all the lands and bring you into your own land. Then I will sprinkle clean water on you, and you will be clean; I will cleanse you from all your filthiness and from all your idols. Moreover, I will give you a new heart and put a new spirit within you; and I will remove the heart of stone from your flesh and give you a heart of flesh. I will put My Spirit within you and cause you to walk in My statutes, and you will be careful to observe My ordinances. You will live in the land that I gave to your forefathers; so you will be My people, and I will be your God.
> (Ezekiel 36:24–28)

Our new hearts come through redemption, when God by his Spirit removes the heart of stone and gives us a heart of flesh (v. 26). God's Spirit dwells within, and this divine heart transplant empowers God's people to walk in God's statutes and be careful to observe God's ordinances (v. 27).

When the prophet Jeremiah described this same

promise, he identified it as the "new covenant":

> "Behold, days are coming," declares the LORD,
> "when I will make a new covenant with the
> house of Israel and with the house of Judah,
> not like the covenant which I made with their
> fathers in the day I took them by the hand
> to bring them out of the land of Egypt, My
> covenant which they broke, although I was
> a husband to them," declares the LORD. "But
> this is the covenant which I will make with
> the house of Israel after those days," declares
> the LORD, "I will put My law within them
> and on their heart I will write it; and I will be
> their God, and they shall be My people. They
> will not teach again, each man his neighbor
> and each man his brother, saying, 'Know the
> LORD,' for they will all know Me, from the
> least of them to the greatest of them," declares
> the LORD, "for I will forgive their iniquity, and
> their sin I will remember no more."
>
> (Jeremiah 31:31–34)

Jeremiah described this promise of the new covenant as God's law written not on tablets of stone but upon the hearts of his people. This new heart in this new covenant would bring with it "forgiveness of sins" and would give the ability to "know the LORD" and walk in his ways. The hope of the new covenant was not associated primarily with the nation of Israel, but with a new people called to salvation from all nations (Romans 1:16; Revelation 7:9–10). How would God fulfill this promise?

## A New Heart is *Possible* through the Gospel of Jesus

God promised to establish the new covenant through a Messiah who would redeem his people and inaugurate it. The message of the New Testament revolves around Jesus as this Messiah. When Jesus's ministry began he declared,

> *The time is fulfilled, and the kingdom of God is at hand; repent and believe in the gospel.*
>
> (Mark 1:15)

The word "gospel" simply means "good news," and the goodness of this news is that Jesus has now come as this promised redeemer to fulfill the new covenant and save his people from their sins (Matthew 1:21).

We see a foretaste of how Jesus would accomplish this during his last Passover meal with his disciples before he was betrayed, convicted, and crucified. While sitting with his disciples Jesus took bread, broke it, gave it to them, and said, "Take it; this is My body" (Mark 14:22). He also took the cup, gave thanks, gave it to them to drink, and said these prophetic words: "This is My blood of the covenant, which is poured out for many" (Mark 14:24). This event that Christians celebrate as the Lord's Supper represents the good news of the gospel: how God, through the shed blood of his own Son, inaugurated the new covenant and redeemed his people.

Jesus, fully human and yet fully God (Hebrews 4:15), lived the perfect life that we cannot live, and died on the cross bearing the wrath of God for our sins in our place (2 Corinthians 5:21). He rose from the dead three days later to give us new life (Romans 4:25), and he now sits at the right hand of the throne of God, ruling over all things (Hebrews 1:3) and interceding as mediator between God and his people (Hebrews 7:25). This gospel declares that, though we are sinners who deserve God's wrath and punishment for our sins resulting from our defiled hearts, we can be forgiven, receive new hearts, be saved from God's judgment, and be given an eternal inheritance. Our salvation is not achieved by anything we have done or will do, but solely by what Jesus has accomplished on our behalf. However, to receive the promises of the new covenant, we must respond to the gospel.

## A New Heart is *Possessed* when We Respond to the Gospel

Though God alone awakens and calls sinners to himself, we have the responsibility to respond to this good news in faith. Through our response of faith, God miraculously transforms our hearts, replacing our defiled hearts with new ones. The biblical response is to

> repent and believe in the gospel.
>
> (Mark 1:15)

As sinners we must see our need for a Savior, repent (i.e. turn) from our sins, and trust in Jesus. Then we can know the Lord, walk in his ways, and desire what God desires. It is precisely this transformation that allows us to be

> dead to sin, but alive to God in Christ Jesus.
>
> (Romans 6:11)

32

Don't be fooled into thinking that the sin of pornography can be overcome by external methods such as a twelve-step program. To destroy pornography's effects on a life we must get to the core of the problem—the defiled, sinful heart. Rooting out the problem begins with the possession of the new heart promised in the new covenant, made possible through the saving work of Jesus and possessed when we turn from our sins to follow Jesus. This new heart, however, must be nurtured and matured if lasting victory over sexual sin is to be achieved. It is to this process and its appropriate context that we now turn.

# The Transformation: The Local Church

Individualism is an approach to life that produces the idea that we do not need anyone or anything. This philosophy, like many ideologies of our culture, has infiltrated the church and has produced a "lone-ranger" approach to the Christian life that is unbiblical and unsuccessful.

Just as a newborn baby must be constantly cared for by others if it is to grow in a healthy, mature manner, so a Christian's new heart must be carefully nurtured if he is to develop and grow in the healthy, biblical way God has designed. This is best done through God's redeemed people in the context of the local church. The church should be central in the guarding of this transformed heart for two main reasons.

*First*, the daily fight against sin is a constant reality. Though Christians possess this new heart and the indwelling of God's spirit, we still live in a fallen world where the attacks of sin, the flesh, and the devil are constant and intense. The daily fight against sin is an intense spiritual battle:

> *For our struggle is not against flesh and blood, but against the rulers, against the powers, against the world forces of this darkness, against the spiritual forces of wickedness in the heavenly places.*
> (Ephesians 6:12)

To try to fight this battle alone is as foolish as a zealous charge by a single soldier on the battlefield. We need others around us in order to fight the battle with sin and the attacks of the enemy. Those appointed warriors have been provided by God through the local church.

*Second*, our propensity to embrace individualism demands the aid of the local church. The mentality that as Christians we do not need anything outside ourselves, including other Christians, to walk through life and fight our struggles with sin is an all-too-common fallacy. For the local church to be involved in our lives as God designs, we must diligently fight against constant cultural messages such as "You're your own man. You don't need anyone else. You're weak if you depend on others." The local church plays a corrective role in the lives of Christians and is especially needed in the battle with pornography. How is the local church to play this role in the individual lives of Christians?

The thrust of this care and accountability begins when the divinely appointed shepherds of a local church (e.g. pastors and elders) minister the Word of God as they

> reprove, rebuke, exhort, with great patience
> and instruction.
> (2 Timothy 4:2; see also 1 Peter 5:1–4)

Those shepherds then facilitate discipleship relationships between weaker members and more mature members who desire to obey the instruction to "Bear one another's burdens" (Galatians 6:2). Consequently, local-church leaders and members are the ones who care most about weaker believers' purity and spiritual growth in Christ. This effort of the local church also preserves the threat of church discipline for anyone who becomes complacent in the task of battling sin (Matthew 18:15–17; 1 Corinthians 5:1–8; 2 Thessalonians 3:14–15). Within this context, there are three main areas that the local church must faithfully address if it is to nurture and mature believers' new hearts in a way that can provide lasting victory over a struggle with pornography.

## Daily Confess and Repent of Sin

A common misconception is that repentance occurs only at the moment we first trust in Christ. However, that moment is simply to be the start of what should become a daily regimen of searching our hearts for sin, confessing it, and repenting of it. Then, by faith, we walk in the freedom of the gospel and the righteousness that is ours in Christ. King David modeled this kind of transparent confession and repentance as he reflected on his affair with Bathsheba:

*Be gracious to me, O God, according to*
  *Your lovingkindness;*
*According to the greatness of Your*
  *compassion blot out my transgressions.*
*Wash me thoroughly from my iniquity*
*And cleanse me from my sin.*
*For I know my transgressions,*
*And my sin is ever before me.*
*Against You, You only, I have sinned*

> And done what is evil in Your sight,
> So that You are justified when You speak
> And blameless when You judge.
>
> (Psalm 51:1–4)

David's confession reflects a confidence in the Lord's compassion and forgiveness based on his unchanging character. How much more should Christians look back at the cross and have confidence in this same compassion and forgiveness! Christians who understand the connection between the merciful grace of God and confession and repentance see what a gift it is to engage in this task daily.

Though repentance involves intensely personal moments of introspection, we should also be prepared to be open about our sin in the context of close, trustworthy relationships we develop with others within our local church. We battle sin with others as we confess our struggles to them. There is a freedom we experience when we not only confess our sins to God, but also make them known to those who care most about the purity of our lives. Through these deliberate conversations, others can often identify sin that exists in our hearts better than we can on our own. In sharing our struggles, we also allow our brothers in Christ to know how specifically to pray for the purity of our lives.

Another important reason to involve others within our local church in this task of daily confession and repentance is the tendency in most of us to hide these kinds of sins. Sexual sins are some of the most embarrassing, shameful, and taboo sins, and yet our hearts and minds are so susceptible to them. We need the other Christians who love us most, who are most involved in our lives, who are willing to say hard things, and who care most about us walking in victory over sin, to walk alongside and help us root out those sins in our hearts. Christians must realize that though we have new hearts and a Spirit-empowered ability to walk in God's ways, we must never underestimate the importance of daily battling sin and involving those who have committed themselves with us to strive for purity and holiness. John Owen affirmed this task to daily battle sin by exhorting every Christian to be "killing sin or it will be killing you."[5]

---

5  John Owen, *Overcoming Sin and Temptation*, ed. by Kelly Kapic and Justin Taylor (Wheaton, IL: Crossway, 2006), 50.

## Put Off Sin and Put On Christ

The principle of putting off sin and putting on Christ is most clearly stated in the apostle Paul's letter to the church in Ephesus:[6]

> ... if indeed you have heard Him and have been taught in Him, just as truth is in Jesus ... in reference to your former manner of life ... lay aside the old self, which is being corrupted in accordance with the lusts of deceit, and ... be renewed in the spirit of your mind, and put on the new self, which in the likeness of God has been created in righteousness and holiness of the truth.
> (Ephesians 4:21–24)

Paul instructs these Christians to "lay aside the old self, which is being corrupted." We are to be renewed in the spirit of our minds by putting on "the new self." This is part of the daily battle with sin, and we need others to help us put off sin and to put on Christ. Since much of this principle to "put off and put on" is rooted in renewing the mind (Ephesians 4:23), the

6   This principle is also found in Colossians 3:8–9; James 1:21; and 1 Peter 2:1–2.

mind must, therefore, be the battleground on which we focus.

I once spoke to a single brother who strongly desired to fight his battle with pornography. He found that, in moments of temptation, he was unsuccessful when he tried to preach to himself repeatedly, "I will not look at this; I will not do this; I will not lust after this woman." Most of us would admit that if we just keep telling ourselves to "not do this or that," that is exactly what we will eventually do. We have to put off, but then also put on. We accomplish this best by taking those sinful thoughts and countering them with thoughts of Christ and his Word. This brother found greater success in battling temptation when he didn't simply tell himself not to look, but also filled his mind with "whatever is true, whatever is honorable, whatever is right, whatever is pure, whatever is lovely, whatever is of good repute" (Philippians 4:8).[7]

---

7  See the Personal Application Projects section for examples of the lies men believe in temptation and God's truth that combats them.

## Embrace Radical Accountability

Integral to putting off sin and putting on Christ is Jesus's radical teaching, from the Sermon on the Mount, about what it truly means to be his disciple. After warning his hearers about committing adultery in the heart as a result of looking at a woman lustfully, Jesus said,

> *If your right eye makes you stumble, tear it out and throw it from you; for it is better for you to lose one of the parts of your body, than for your whole body to be thrown into hell. If your right hand makes you stumble, cut it off and throw it from you; for it is better for you to lose one of the parts of your body, than for your whole body to go into hell.*
>
> (Matthew 5:29–30)

Matthew's teaching, which is exaggerated (hyperbolic) and not meant to be taken literally, is emphatic: be radical in the fight against sin. Because it is especially easy to become entangled in sexual sin, Paul says we are to

> abstain from sexual immorality.
> (1 Thessalonians 4:3; see also 1 Corinthians 6:18)

A very effective way to keep from stumbling is to implement radical accountability. In the context of pornography and other forms of sexual sin, this can be defined as setting up unshakable barriers of access,[8] which seems extreme to a non-Christian but is necessary to ensure purity.

The most radical accountability will be merely frustrating, legalistic, and ineffective behavior modification without the context of the local church nurturing and maturing a new heart. Nevertheless, radical accountability can ensure protection from a moment of weakness and provide opportunities to effectively address the sins of the heart that produce that weakness.

Finally, let's consider a real example of how my church had the privilege of nurturing and maturing the new heart of a single brother who had a major struggle with viewing pornography on the Internet. This man came to the pastors, confessed his sinful struggle, and said he would do whatever we asked of him in the pursuit of repentance and victory over this struggle. The first thing we did was go to his house, take his computer from him, and instruct

---

8  Examples are canceling Internet services, or a wife creating the passwords for Internet or cable channel access.

him to cancel his Internet access first thing the next morning *(radical accountability)*. He spent some time meeting with one of the pastors, trying to discover the desires of his heart that led to this behavior. As those sins were discovered, that pastor led him to create a daily pattern of confessing those sins to God and this pastor *(daily confession and repentance)* and finding the forgiveness that we are promised through Christ in his Word:

> *If we confess our sins, He is faithful and*
> *righteous to forgive us our sins and to*
> *cleanse us from all unrighteousness.*
>
> (1 John 1:9)

Then the pastors appointed two reliable, trustworthy, and mature Christian brothers from our church to meet weekly with him for prayer, encouragement, and self-examination. Their task was to teach him how to recognize the sinful desires of his heart that brought the temptation and sinful thoughts, and how to combat those sinful thoughts with Scripture and thoughts of our Savior *(putting off sin and putting on Christ)*.

By God's grace, this man found lasting victory over his struggle, and he continues to walk in that victory.

As pastors we strongly believe that if we had skipped any of these three steps in pursuing his restoration, we would not have experienced the same result. The new hearts that God has given us, his Spirit who dwells within us, and his law that is written on our hearts, are all we need to be transformed into new creatures in Christ (2 Corinthians 5:17). We should not overlook, however, the divinely designed essential role that other brothers and sisters in Christ within our local church play in helping us to find lasting victory over sin, especially the sinful struggles that accompany pornography.

## A Case Study

This booklet argues that the most effective way to overcome devastating bondage to a sin like pornography is through a heart changed by the power of the gospel and through the impact of submission and commitment to a group of other Christians within a local church. To conclude I want to chronicle a real-life marriage that experienced the pain and despair of this sinful struggle, yet found hope in the gospel and help in the local church. Real names have been changed and specifics unimportant to this discussion have been generalized. I pray it will give "legs" to this work and give hope to you and others as you seek to apply these principles in your unique situation.

My church was very excited when Jim and Linda began to visit us. They came from a healthy, vibrant church where they had grown in their faith, and upon their move to Louisville they sought a local church that would continue to care for and shepherd them as they had previously experienced. This couple modeled so much of the trust, affection, commitment, and graciousness that we desire for all marriages in the church, which is why I was curious when Jim, soon after becoming a member, requested that I come to his house to meet him to discuss a struggle with sin that was affecting his marriage. As I met with him, Jim confessed his struggle with viewing pornography. He had struggled with this behavior in the past, but now, after a season of obedience, he had relapsed into this old way of sin. He had recently confessed his struggle to Linda, which had led to this invitation for me to meet with him for counsel and help. I was reminded that the evidence of a strong and godly marriage is not the absence of sinful struggles, but how husband and wife choose to deal with the hurt and pain that accompanies these kinds of struggles.

Jim's issues of the heart were on full display for myself and his wife, and radical accountability was put in place by the pastors using other men from our church. Through realizing the gravity of his sin, Jim learned how to be loving and patient as his wife dealt with the pain his behavior caused her. The church also helped Linda deal with the hurt, bitterness, feelings of unattractiveness, and broken trust that always accompany this betrayal. She was pastorally directed to another woman in the church who was carefully chosen to help her deal with the hurt and embrace the essential role God had given her to serve her husband through this struggle, help protect her marriage, and find the freedom of forgiveness. Additionally, the pastors and members involved prayed diligently for Jim and Linda.

By God's grace, Jim and Linda now flourish in our church as leaders; they represent a model of a faithful and healthy marriage to others, and they rejoice in the manner God has used this struggle to strengthen their marriage and display how the power of the gospel works in the hearts of God's people to overcome sin. They are a primary resource to whom our pastors send other couples who are struggling in a similar way.

This testimony does not mean the struggle has ended for them. The enemy loves to attack marriages in their most vulnerable places. Their hearts must be consistently searched for sin, their efforts to put off sin and put on Christ must be diligent, and accountability must remain in place. Yet this couple remains a model for our church of how the gospel can powerfully change both husband and wife as they stay committed to Christ and each other, submit themselves to the authority, care, and counsel of God's Word and the local church, and trust in the power of God to work all things for the good of his people and the glory of his great name!

## Personal Application Projects

### For Hurting Wives

Many are hurt by a man's struggle with pornography, but no one more than the man's wife. The feelings of hurt, betrayal, and distrust that a wife experiences toward her husband because of this struggle are very similar to those that come with adultery. The gospel is the only hope for a man to find victory over this bondage and the only way a wife who has been deeply hurt by her husband can find forgiveness and reestablish trust.

Thus, the work to restore trust and intimacy within a marriage deeply affected by this sinful struggle is possible through the gospel and is applied most effectively within the local church. Nevertheless, it takes a diligent, patient, and gracious effort on the part of both husband and wife. Here are six practical ways a wife can help her struggling husband and find forgiveness toward him in the process.

1. *She must embrace the fact that she plays an important role of accountability for her husband.* The wife may be tempted to distance herself from helping her husband and, thus, rely on other men to play that role. However, the wife is an important source of accountability for her husband. She knows him better than anyone, cares more than anyone that he overcomes this struggle, and is the object of the husband's greatest affection. Urge the wife not to be afraid to play this role. She becomes a great asset for her husband in overcoming this struggle.

2. *She must know that this is not her fault. (It really isn't her; it's him.)* Ironically, when a husband chooses to sin in this way, a wife will often blame herself. She was not attractive enough, did not show him enough attention, or did not see the warning signs. The fact is that we are all responsible before God for our own sinful hearts. An unhealthy marriage can be a breeding ground for this struggle for a husband, but the wife should never feel the responsibility for his sinful decisions.

3.   *She must share her hurt with him.* Encourage the wife not to hesitate to share how his sinful actions have made her feel. It will remind the husband of one of many reasons why he should never allow this destructive pattern to return. It also acts as a healthy and good way for the wife to grieve through the hurt and find forgiveness for him.

4.   *She must seek counsel and care from another godly woman.* If possible, put the betrayed wife in the care of another godly woman who has walked through this or a similar struggle. Choose carefully, however, as this is meant to help the wife find empathy, grace, and forgiveness toward her husband, not become an opportunity to fuel the fire of hurt and bitterness that already exists.

5.   *She must guard her heart against bitterness.* Bitterness is an all-too-common response to the offenses of others against us. The best way to help a wife harmed by sexual sins guard against bitterness is to remind her of the gospel and how God has forgiven her sins. Keep before her her need for repentance and God's promise of forgiveness, and God will provide the grace needed to forgive her husband.

6. *She must pursue regular sexual intimacy with her husband.* The best thing for a hurting wife to do is the last thing she feels like doing after being hurt in this way: pursue sexual intimacy with her husband (1 Corinthians 7:5). This intentional intimacy acts as a safeguard for this particular struggle in a husband and will break down the barriers to intimacy that the enemy wants to keep up as long as possible.

May the Lord give you grace as you attempt to care for a wife who certainly needs care after this sort of betrayal. Remember, the gospel is powerful enough to restore any marriage from the deepest damage caused by sexual sin, and God powerfully uses the local church to care for those affected.

*APPLICATION QUESTIONS FOR WIVES*

1. Is there anything keeping you from embracing your important role of accountability for your husband? If so, what?

2. Is there any unforgiveness, bitterness, or anger you need to share with your husband?

3. Can you articulate the reason(s) why you do not desire physical intimacy with your husband?

53

4. How has the gospel given you hope during this time?

## For Recovering Husbands

The work to restore trust and intimacy within a marriage deeply affected by this sinful struggle is only possible through the gospel and is applied most effectively within the local church. Here are six practical ways that a husband can reestablish trust and intimacy with his hurting wife.

1. *He must be patient toward his hurting wife.* Men are known to deal with something, then move on. A wife, especially one sinned against by pornography, will not move on so quickly. A wife does not get past this offense in the same amount of time a husband often expects she should. Encourage the husband to be patient with his wife as she tries to find forgiveness and reestablish trust. By God's grace it will happen—but in time.

2. *He must understand the seriousness of his sin against her.* Sexual sin hurts a wife more deeply than most other sins against her. A husband

54

needs to realize that the reason why this sin stings so much is that it seems to confirm almost every doubt and insecurity most women already battle within themselves. Understanding the seriousness of this sin and the pain it causes will help cultivate patience and prevent a recurrence of it.

3. *He must look to his wife to play an important role of accountability.* It is easy to seek the accountability of another man when it comes to this struggle because, he might say, "Only another man knows what the battle is like." Yet he does not have to sleep next to that man every night. He does not have to look into his eyes, knowing the hurt he caused. He does not have to be as patient and gracious with his buddy as he must be with his wife. It may need to be in the context of regular counseling for a while, but convince him that his wife will be a great asset in establishing his new patterns and in protecting him from falling again.

4. *He must consistently and creatively romance his wife.* A husband should have already been pursuing his wife romantically as a regular practice. Now he must understand that this

pattern must be established to restore his marriage. Sexual sin attacks a wife's confidence and security that her husband loves and desires her. This confidence is a must for a healthy marriage and remains so for one needing to be restored.

5. *He must affirm his physical attraction to her.* It should surprise no man that when he looks at other women in lustful ways, it will communicate a sharp message to his wife that he does not find her attractive. Most men would confess that that is not what drove them to pornography, but it is inescapable that this is how a wife feels because of it. Encourage the man verbally to affirm his physical attraction to his wife. Then he must back it up with his actions.

6. *He must realize that the battle never ends this side of eternity.* The gospel is powerful to free men from this bondage and to establish new patterns in their lives, but the fences of accountability must always remain. Most of the men who slip up in this area do so just when they start getting confident that they no longer struggle with pornography (1 Corinthians 10:12). The guards come down. The wife has forgiven

him. The accountability partner has not asked about the struggle for a while. The gradual decline of these forms of accountability should act as a warning sign and a reminder that this struggle in our sex-saturated culture will only end when the perfectly faithful husband, Christ, gathers his bride to himself (Revelation 19:6–9).

May the Lord grant you wisdom as you work with husbands who struggle in this way so that the patterns are broken, marriages are mended, and the power of Christ is credited.

### APPLICATION QUESTIONS FOR HUSBANDS

1. Are you hesitant to allow your wife to play a major role in your accountability? Why or why not?

2. What is your deliberate plan of action to romance your wife, affirm your physical attraction to her, and win back her trust?

3. Do you find yourself growing in patience or impatience toward your wife's hurt? Why?

4. What is keeping you from being solely satisfied in your wife (Proverbs 5:19)?

### Putting Off Sin & Putting On Christ

| Common Lies Men Believe in Times of Temptation | Truths Men Must Believe in Times of Temptation |
| --- | --- |
| "I will be the only one affected by this action. It doesn't directly affect anyone else." | My sin is against a holy God and it took the death of Christ to pay for it. Ps. 51:4; Rom. 5:8–10. |
| "I will only do it this one time." | Christ died so that I may live a life free from all sin and pursue holiness. Rom. 6:1; Eph. 5:3; James 2:10. |
| "Since my wife doesn't satisfy me in this way, I need to satisfy myself." "I don't have a wife to bring me fulfillment, so I need to fulfill myself." | Sexual pleasure must come through my wife only. Prov. 5:19. My marriage is not about me; it is about loving my wife as Christ loves the church. 1 Cor. 7; Eph. 5:25. Singleness is not about me; it is about glorifying God in my body. 1 Thes. 4:3–5. |
| "It will feel good and bring pleasure and fulfillment." | Sin cannot bring lasting pleasure; Christ brings true and lasting pleasure. Heb. 11:24–26. |
| "I'll just browse on the computer and see what happens." | Flirting with sin leads to destruction; following Christ leads to life. Prov. 5:8; Prov. 7:21–23; 1 Cor. 6:18. |

| | |
|---|---|
| "No one will ever find out." | It is more satisfying to please my all-knowing Father than to secretly indulge my sin. Num. 32:23; Ps. 90:8; Prov. 5:21; Heb. 13:4; Heb. 4:12–13. |
| "I'm going to do it anyway, so let me just get it over with." | Christ died and has given me his Spirit to resist all temptation. Ezek. 36:24–32; 1 Cor. 10:13; 1 Tim. 6:11–12; 2 Tim. 2:22. |
| "It's really not that big a deal." | It took the death of the Son of God to free me of this sin. Rom. 5:8–10.<br><br>Indulging sin leads to destruction; persevering in faith leads to life. Matt. 5:27–30; Matt. 18:7–9; Heb. 13:4. |
| "God is going to forgive me anyway." | God's grace gives me the power to resist sin, not to pursue it. Rom. 6:1; Rom. 2:4.<br><br>God will judge my sin but reward my obedience. Heb. 13:4. |
| "I can use a little break or relief." | Relief will come when the war with sin is over and I will see my Savior in all his glory. Phil. 3:12; Rev. 7:9–12; 21:3–4. |

| | |
|---|---|
| "There might be something new I'll be missing out on or haven't seen yet." | I will always regret gratifying my sin; I will never regret obedience to Christ. Heb. 11:24–26. |
| "If only my wife looked like what I see on the Internet, then I would be satisfied." | My wife is a gift from God and I am to cherish her as Christ cherishes me. Prov. 5:15–20; Eph. 5:25. |
| "I am a man; it's natural and I can't help it." | I am a new man in Christ who can flee sin and pursue righteousness. 1 Thes. 4:3–8; 1 Tim. 6:11. |
| "God created me this way." | I am a new creature in Christ; I do not have to settle for this sin. 2 Cor. 5:17. |
| "I am not sinning as long as I do not physically commit the act." | Sin begins in the heart, but God has given me a new heart to please him. Jer. 31:31–34; Ezek. 36:24–32; Matt. 5:27–30. |
| "I'm bored and have nothing else to do." | The Lord has purchased my life with the death of his Son; I will use my time for his glory. Prov. 5:22–23; Eph. 5:15–16; James 4:13–17. |

*APPLICATION QUESTIONS FOR MEN*

1. Which lie(s) are you most tempted to believe at the moment of temptation?

2. Are you daily making the effort to root out sin and speak God's Word to yourself?

3. What truth(s) from God's Word are you struggling to believe the most?

4. What steps of radical accountability have you put in place as you daily put off sin and put on Christ?

## Where Can I Get Further Help?

### Free Online Resources

Challies, Tim, *Sexual Detox: A Guide for the Single Guy* (free eBook), at: http://www.challies.com/sites/all/files/attachments/sexual-detox-a-guide-for-the-single-guy.pdf

Challies, Tim, *Sexual Detox: A Guide for the Married Guy* (free eBook), at: http://www.challies.com/sites/all/files/attachments/sexual-detox-a-guide-for-the-married-guy.pdf

Powlison, David, "Breaking Pornography Addiction," Part 1, at: http://www.ccef.org/breaking-pornography-addiction-part-1

Powlison, David, "Breaking Pornography Addiction," Part 2, at: http://ccef.org/breaking-pornography-addiction-part-two

Taylor, Justin, lists several online resources: http://thegospelcoalition.org/blogs/justintaylor/2009/12/11/porndemic/

The author also deals with issues of pornography on his blog "Practical Shepherding," at: www.practicalshepherding.com

## Books

Challies, Tim, *Sexual Detox: A Guide for Guys Who Are Sick of Porn* (Adelphi, MD: Cruciform Press, 2010)

Harris, Joshua, *Sex Is Not the Problem (Lust Is): Sexual Purity in a Lust-Saturated World* (Colorado Springs: Multnomah, 2003)

Struthers, William M., *Wired for Intimacy: How Pornography Hijacks the Male Brain* (Downers Grove, IL: Intervarsity Press, 2009)

Owen, John, *The Mortification of Sin* (Edinburgh: Banner of Truth, 2004)

## Books in the Help! series include …

Help! Someone I Love Has Cancer (Howard)
  ISBN 978-1-84625-217-4

Help! My Baby Has Died (Weems)
  ISBN 978-1-84625-215-0

Help! My Spouse Has Been Unfaithful (Summers)
  ISBN 978-1-84625-220-4

Help! I Have Breast Cancer (Frields)
  ISBN 978-1-84625-216-7

Help! My Marriage Has Grown Cold (Thomas)
  ISBN 978-1-84625-219-8

Help! He's Struggling with Pornography (Croft)
  ISBN 978-1-84625-218-1

Help! My Toddler Rules the House (Tautges)
  ISBN 978-1-84625-221-1

Help! Someone I Love Has Been Abused
(Newheiser)
  ISBN 978-1-84625-222-8

(More titles in preparation)